POSITIONS ON THE TEAM

POSITIONS IN FOOTBALL

EMMETT MARTIN

PowerKiDS press

New York

Published in 2023 by The Rosen Publishing Group, Inc.
29 East 21st Street, New York, NY 10010

Portions of this work were originally authored by Ryan Nagelhout and published as *Football: Who Does What?* All new material in this edition was authored by Emmett Martin.

Editor: Therese Shea
Book Design: Michael Flynn

Photo Credits: Cover (football) Mtsaride/Shutterstock.com; (series jersey texture) Kwangmoozaa/Shutterstock.com; cover (grass texture) comzeal images/Shutterstock.com; cover (basketball play) Dejan Popovic/Shutterstock.com; p. 5 Alesandro14/Shutterstock.com; p. 7 (all) Mike Orlov/Shutterstock.com; p. 9 Artur Didyk/Shutterstock.com; p. 10 Eugene Onischenko/Shutterstock.com; p. 11 masisyan/Shutterstock.com; p. 12 Melinda Nagy/Shutterstock.com; pp. 13, 21, 24 JoeSAPhotos/Shutterstock.com; pp. 15 (all), 19 Alex Kravtsov/Shutterstock.com; p. 17 (inset) Master1305/Shutterstock.com; p. 17 (main) Sergey Mironov/Shutterstock.com; p. 20 Haslam Photography/Shutterstock.com; p. 23 Steve Jacobson/Shutterstock.com; p. 25 Sergey Nivens/Sutterstock.com; p. 27 Paul Spinelli/AP Photo; p. 29 Ben Margot/AP Photo.

Library of Congress Cataloging-in-Publication Data

Names: Martin, Emmett, author.
Title: Positions in football / Emmett Martin.
Description: New York : PowerKids Press, [2023] | Series: Positions on the team | Includes index.
Identifiers: LCCN 2021062501 (print) | LCCN 2021062502 (ebook) | ISBN 9781538387030 (library binding) | ISBN 9781538387016 (paperback) | ISBN 9781538387023 (set) | ISBN 9781538387047 (ebook)
Subjects: LCSH: Football–United States–Juvenile literature. | Football–United States–Terminology–Juvenile literature.
Classification: LCC GV950.7 .M268 2023 (print) | LCC GV950.7 (ebook) | DDC 796.332/2–dc23/eng/20220110
LC record available at https://lccn.loc.gov/2021062501
LC ebook record available at https://lccn.loc.gov/2021062502

Manufactured in the United States of America

Some of the images in this book illustrate individuals who are models. The depictions do not imply actual situations or events.

CPSIA Compliance Information: Batch #CSPK23. For Further Information contact Rosen Publishing, New York, New York at 1-800-237-9932.

CONTENTS

OFFENSE OR DEFENSE?

A winning football team has a good offense *and* a good defense. Offensive players aim to score points, while defensive players try to stop the other team from scoring. Both offense and defense have a lot of different positions.

Football is a fast game, and every position is an important one. Many people have an idea about what a quarterback does. However, they might not know the difference between a free safety and a strong safety or what positions are involved in special teams. Do you? You will after reading this book! Let's learn more about the positions that make up an American football team.

PLAY IT SAFE

No matter the position on the field, every football player needs to do their job safely. Always wear safety equipment, including a helmet and pads, when you're playing football. Listen to your coaches. They can teach you the right way to tackle, or hit another player. Make sure you, your teammates, and the players on the other team stay safe.

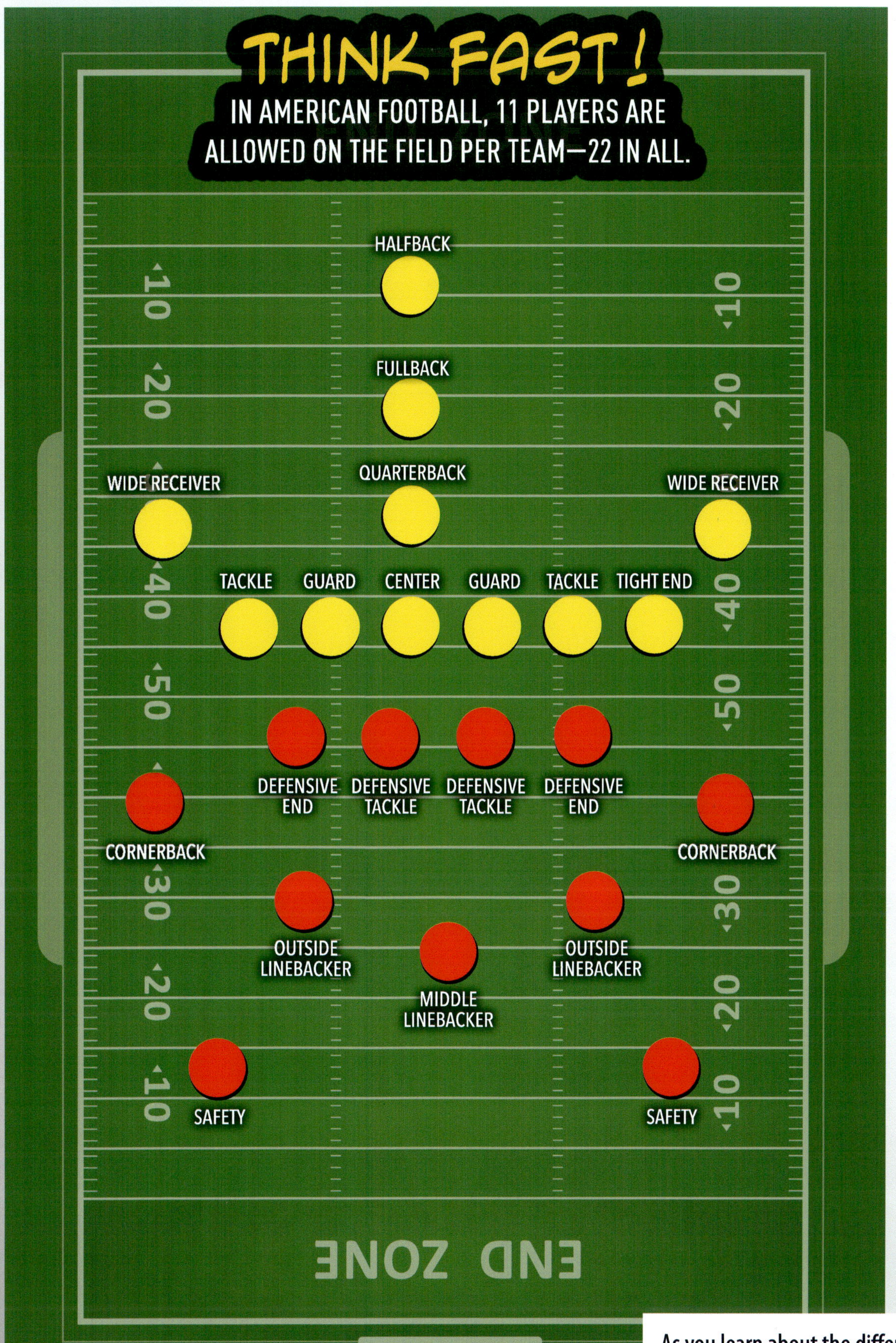

As you learn about the different positions in American football, look back to this page to see where each player may start on the field.

THE QUARTERBACK LEADS

Most people think the quarterback has the most important position in football. A quarterback's job is to direct a team's offense down the field to score points. Quarterbacks run the offense and are commonly the first to touch the football after the **snap**.

Quarterbacks need to think quickly. Some quarterbacks call the plays a team runs on offense. They need to change plays to suit different situations in the game. They often base decisions on what the other team's defense is doing. Quarterbacks must make plays while avoiding the opponent's defense, which wants to tackle them and make them lose the football.

QUICK ON THEIR FEET

Quarterbacks don't always have to throw the football–they can run with it! Today's best quarterbacks make thrilling plays with their feet and with their arms. A running quarterback needs to be able to scramble well, which means get away from the defense even if their offensive protection can't guard them.

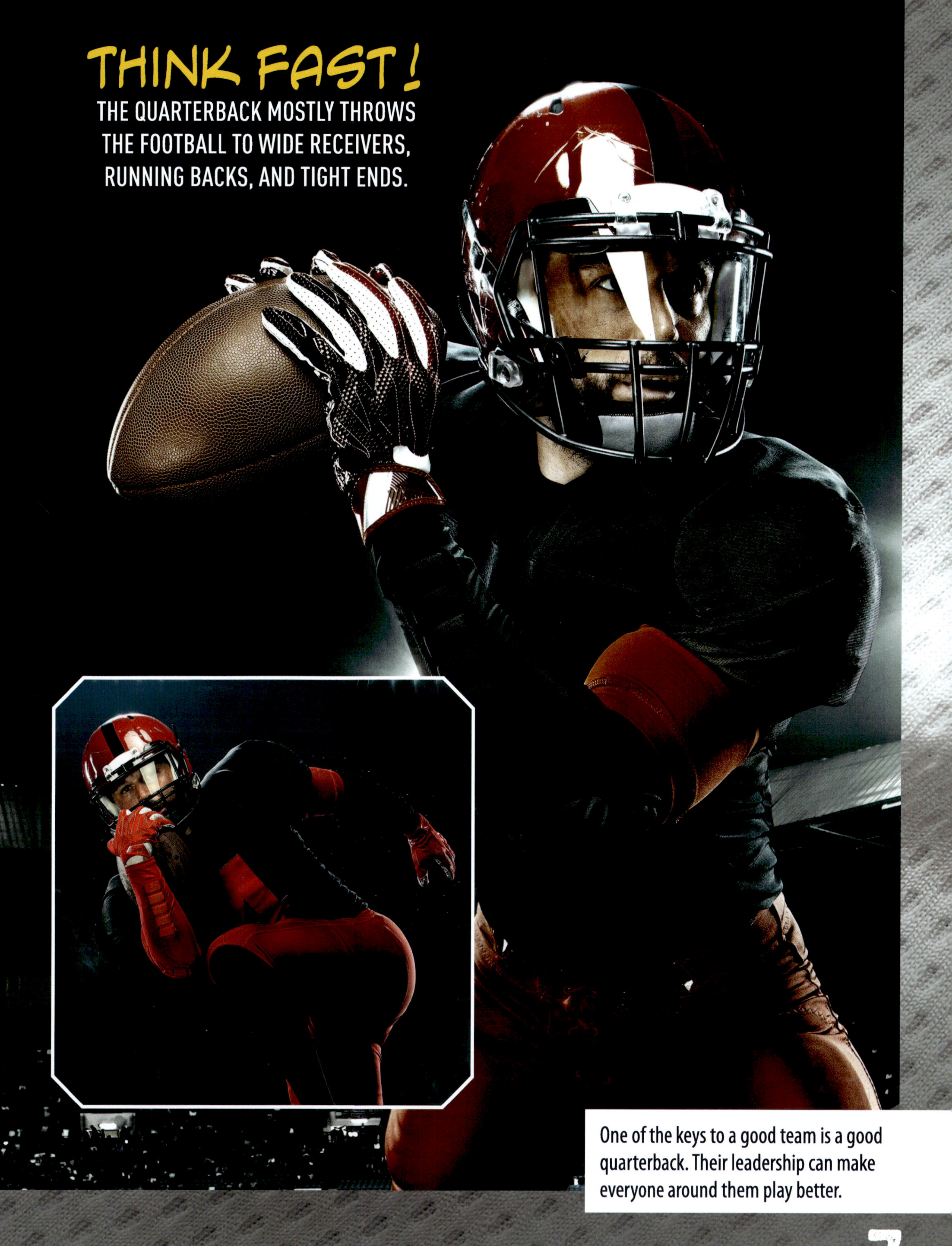

THINK FAST!

THE QUARTERBACK MOSTLY THROWS THE FOOTBALL TO WIDE RECEIVERS, RUNNING BACKS, AND TIGHT ENDS.

One of the keys to a good team is a good quarterback. Their leadership can make everyone around them play better.

THE OFFENSIVE LINE

The biggest players on the team usually make up the offensive line. Their job is to keep the other team's defense from tackling players on their team who have the football. Often they stay near or behind the line of scrimmage. That's the imaginary line on the field where all offensive plays start.

There are five different offensive line positions. The center plays the middle of the offensive line. Centers snap the football, usually to a quarterback, to start a play. The left and right guards play on each side of the center. The left and right tackles play on the ends of the offensive line.

GUARDING THE BLIND SIDE

The most important offensive line player is whomever is protecting the quarterback's blind side. If the quarterback is left-handed, it's the right tackle. If the quarterback is right-handed, it's the left tackle. This player keeps the defense from hitting the quarterback when the quarterback is trying to throw the ball. Quarterbacks often can't see the defense coming from their blind side.

THINK FAST!

THE OFFENSIVE LINE TRIES TO CREATE A PROTECTED AREA FOR THEIR QUARTERBACK TO THROW THE BALL. IT'S CALLED THE POCKET.

The offensive line may start this way on the field. The offensive line blocks defenders so they can't reach the football.

SPEEDY RUNNING BACKS

The running back is another important offensive position in football. This player's job is to run the football. Before the snap, they line up behind or next to the quarterback. When a running back is given the football on a running play, it's called a handoff.

HALFBACK OR FULLBACK?

Running backs are sometimes called halfbacks, but another kind of running back is the fullback. Fullbacks also stand behind the quarterback, but often don't run with the football. Instead, they run to meet defenders and block them for the quarterback or the other running back. Some fullbacks catch passes, but many are used to block farther down the field.

Running backs are fast runners and have good hands. They might also catch passes from the quarterback. They must be able to see spaces on the field to run through that blockers have created. Some running backs are big and can bowl over defenders. Other running backs run past the defense or stop and start to make defensive players miss the tackle.

THINK FAST!

WHEN RUNNING BACKS OR OTHER OFFENSIVE PLAYERS LOSE THE BALL BEFORE BEING TACKLED, IT'S CALLED A FUMBLE.

Since running backs are runners, teams often have a few people in this position to allow players to rest when needed.

TARGETING WIDE RECEIVERS

A wide receiver is the chief target for a quarterback's forward passes. Each wide receiver stands away from the offensive line and near the sidelines. Wide receivers run to certain places on the field to catch the quarterback's throw.

ALL LINED UP

Most passing plays put at least one wide receiver on each side of the offensive line. But some plays put three on the same side. This is called a trips formation. Sometimes, all three receivers run different routes to make themselves available to catch the ball. But two receivers may block for the player that catches the ball.

Where they run is decided by the play their team runs on offense. The pattern or path a wide receiver runs is called a route. Wide receivers work closely with quarterbacks to complete passes and move the ball down the field. Wide receivers must have great ball-handling skills to catch tough throws and great speed to be fast enough to beat defenders.

THINK FAST!

WIDE RECEIVERS ARE ALSO CALLED WIDEOUTS.

Wide receivers must have both speed and **agility** to get away from the defense and get open to catch a pass.

TIGHT ENDS MIX IT UP

Tight ends are sometimes called a hybrid, or mix, of wide receiver and offensive line. Tight ends, too, catch passes, but they're often bigger and stronger than wide receivers. They need to be because they may start plays on the left or right side of an offensive line and help them block for running plays.

On passing plays, tight ends run routes just like wide receivers. They have to be able to get away from bigger defenders if they want to catch a pass. They need to be smart because they're always in the middle of the action!

TWO-SPORT STARS

An effective tight end is hard for a defensive player to tackle. A tight end's size, strength, and speed make them **formidable** opponents on the field in today's modern football game. These **characteristics** are key in other sports too. In fact, several great NFL (National Football League) tight ends played basketball growing up–including Antonio Gates and Rob Gronkowski.

THINK FAST!

WHERE THE TIGHT END LINES UP MAY GIVE THE DEFENSE AN IDEA OF THE PLAY, BUT SOMETIMES THEIR POSITION ON THE FIELD IS A TRICK!

It can be hard for a defense to know what a tight end will do—go out for a pass or make a block.

THE DEFENSIVE LINE

A football defense has two jobs: stop the other team from scoring and get the ball. Defensive positions are mostly about matching up with the offense and getting in the way. This starts with the defensive line, which stands opposite the offensive line on the line of scrimmage.

The defensive line has two main positions: defensive end and defensive tackle. Tackles play in the middle of the line, and defensive ends play at the ends. The defensive line's job is to get past offensive blockers and tackle the ball carrier. They want to get to the quarterback before a successful throw can happen or tackle the player who has the ball.

THE MAGIC NUMBER?

There are two major types of defense in football. Their names come from the number of players a team puts on the defensive line. If a defense has two defensive ends and two defensive tackles, they run a 4-3 **scheme** because they have a four-player defensive front and three linebackers. If they have a three-player defensive front and four linebackers, they have a 3-4 defense.

If the defense tackles the quarterback behind the line of scrimmage before the quarterback can throw a pass, it's called a sack.

THINK FAST!

PLAYERS ON THE DEFENSIVE LINE ARE SOMETIMES CALLED LINEMEN, BUT WOMEN PLAY FOOTBALL TOO.

LINEBACKERS BACK THE LINE

Linebackers are defensive players who try to stop the offense from running and passing the ball. They "back" the defensive line and often play in groups of three or four. Linebackers are usually faster and smaller than defensive line players because they need to cover more ground on the field.

Depending on the play, a linebacker can rush the quarterback, cover a tight end, or track down a speedy running back. Linebackers need to be able to react quickly to changing plays. An offense will attempt to get these players out of position so they can get by them and make a big play.

PLENTY OF POSITIONS

Linebackers have different positions just like the players on the defensive line do. Outside linebackers start plays behind defensive ends. Inside linebackers, also called middle linebackers, play in the middle of the field. In a 4–3 defense, the positions are middle linebacker, strong-side linebacker (on the side with the most offensive players or the tight end), and weak-side linebacker (on the side with the fewest offensive players).

THINK FAST!

THE SPACE BETWEEN EACH PLAYER ON THE OFFENSIVE LINE IS CALLED A GAP. LINEBACKERS TRY TO FILL THESE GAPS SO THE OFFENSE CAN'T RUN THE BALL THROUGH THEM.

Linebackers often lead a team in tackles. They also try to **blitz** the passer.

CORNERBACKS COVER

A cornerback can be a wide receiver's worst nightmare. Cornerbacks face off against wide receivers on every play. The cornerbacks' job is to cover the receivers, so they aren't open for the quarterback's pass. A long throw from the quarterback to the wide receiver can result in a big gain for the offense. If a pass does come, a cornerback tries to catch it. This is called an interception.

Cornerbacks also help linebackers fill in the gaps to stop running backs from carrying the ball up the field. Cornerbacks need to be fast and have great **reflexes**.

PREVENTING PENALTIES

Cornerbacks must be careful not to take penalties while they're defending wide receivers. A **pass interference** penalty can give the offense the ball at the spot where the penalty occurred, without a catch. That can be a gain of many yards. Football has lots of rules like this that defenses have to follow.

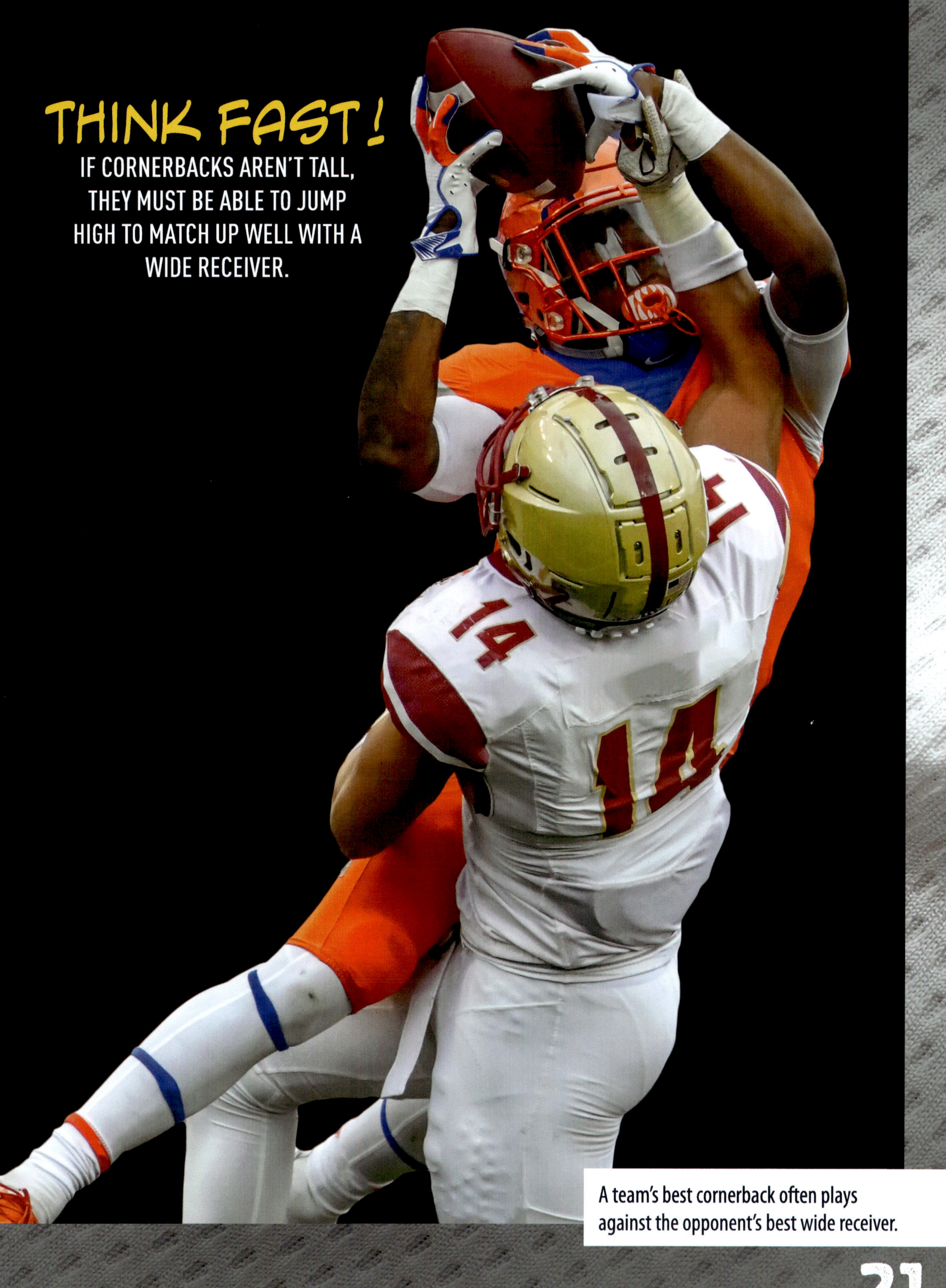

THINK FAST!

IF CORNERBACKS AREN'T TALL, THEY MUST BE ABLE TO JUMP HIGH TO MATCH UP WELL WITH A WIDE RECEIVER.

A team's best cornerback often plays against the opponent's best wide receiver.

SAFETIES AT LAST

The safety is the last chance for the defense to stop the football. Safeties may start way back from the line of scrimmage and wait for the play to come to them. Some safeties read a play and run up to the line of scrimmage to help cover or even tackle a running back. Others race to sack the quarterback.

Most safeties help out cornerbacks and linebackers who are covering players the quarterback may throw to. The safety may cover a wide receiver if the receiver runs to a certain place on the field. That means safeties need to be ready to intercept any deep passes meant for these high-speed offensive players.

FREE AND STRONG

In American football, there are two safety positions on the field, sometimes called the free safety and the strong safety. The strong safety plays opposite the offense's "strong" side, or the side where the tight end lines up, closer to the line of scrimmage. Free safeties, meanwhile, hang back and worry about the passing game. Strong safeties are often bigger than free safeties.

THINK FAST!

A SAFETY IS ALSO THE TERM FOR A PLAY IN AMERICAN FOOTBALL IN WHICH THE SCORING TEAM RECEIVES TWO POINTS. IN CANADIAN FOOTBALL, IT'S CALLED A SAFETY TOUCH.

Safeties may be unblocked since they're farther from the line of scrimmage. They can make a big play when needed.

KICKERS SCORE

One of the most important positions in football is placekicker, or just kicker. These players try to kick the ball between the goal posts at the end of the field. Their job is to score field goals, which are worth three points, and an extra point after every touchdown.

PUNTERS

Punters are a different kind of kicker. They receive the snapped ball from the line of scrimmage and punt, or kick, the football down the field to the opposing team. A good punt forces the team receiving the kick to start as far as possible from the kicking team's end zone. Offenses that can't get **first downs** use their punters a lot.

Placekickers need to be **accurate**. It takes a lot of practice to learn how to kick a football the right way. If the kick is too wide to the right or left, the ball won't make it through the posts. If it's too low, the other team might block the kick.

Kickers often lead their team in scoring each year. Their efforts can be the difference between a win and a loss in a close game.

SPECIAL TEAMS

Special teams are units that are on the field mostly during kicking plays. The groups include the kick off unit; the punting unit; the punt return and kick off return unit; and the field goal and extra point unit.

Special teams players are often backups on offense and defense, but they still have key jobs. They work together to make sure they know what each player needs to do on a play, such as blocking in a certain spot or returning a kick or punt using a particular route. A special teams mistake can cost a team a win!

TRICKS OF THE SPECIAL TEAMS

An onside kick is a short kickoff made on purpose to help the kicking team regain possession of the ball. The ball must be kicked at least 10 yards. Other special teams may try fake punts or field goals after which they run or throw for a first down instead of kicking the ball away.

THINK FAST!

AN ONSIDE KICK IS RISKY FOR THE KICKING TEAM. IF THE OTHER TEAM GETS THE BALL, THEY'RE IN A GOOD POSITION TO SCORE.

Kick and punt returners are often the fastest players on a football team.

STUDY THE PLAYBOOK

You now know about the basic positions in football. It's time to open the playbook and study! There are plenty of ways to get down the field to score. Did you know a running back or wide receiver can throw a pass like a quarterback? A player behind the line of scrimmage can throw a forward pass. They can even throw it to the quarterback. And a player on the offensive line can catch a pass if the ball has been touched by the defense.

Keep watching and playing football to see what else you can learn about this fast-paced, fun sport.

COUNTING ON THE COACH

Some of the most important decision makers in football aren't players–they're coaches. They tell players how best to play their positions. A team in the NFL has a lot of assistant coaches, with a head coach to oversee them. Coaches need to figure out the best plays to use against each **unique** opponent.

In 2015, Jen Welter became the first woman hired to coach in the NFL. In the 2021–2022 season, 12 NFL coaches were women.

GLOSSARY

accurate: Free of mistakes.

agility: The ability to move around quickly and easily.

blitz: In American football, to rush to tackle the passer.

characteristic: A quality that makes a person, thing, or group different from others.

first down: A gain of 10 yards in football in four or fewer plays.

formidable: Having great strength, size, or ability.

NCAA: Stands for the National Collegiate Athletic Association. The organization that governs college sports in the United States.

pass interference: The act of making illegal contact with a player trying to complete a fair catch.

reflex: An action or movement of the body that happens automatically as a reaction to something.

scheme: A plan to accomplish something.

snap: The action of passing the ball back to the quarterback behind the line of scrimmage.

unique: Special or different from anything else.

FOR MORE INFORMATION

BOOKS

Doeden, Matt. *Game Day Football: An Interactive Sports Story.* North Mankato, MN: Capstone Press, 2021.

Hewson, Anthony K. *Football Records*. Lake Elmo, MN: Focus Readers, 2021.

Levit, Joseph. *G.O.A.T. Football Teams*. Minneapolis, MN: Lerner Publications, 2021.

WEBSITES

Football: Player Positions
ducksters.com/sports/footballplayerpositions.php
Figure out if you want to play on the offense, defense, or special teams.

Rookie's Guide
operations.nfl.com/learn-the-game/nfl-basics/rookies-guide/
Find everything you need to understand NFL football.

WFA
wfaprofootball.com/
Check in on the latest news from the Women's Football Alliance (WFA).

INDEX